ADVENTURES IN UNPLUGGED CODING

_ □ X

CODING
WITH
OUTER SPACE

BY KYLIE BURNS

Express!

BELLWETHER MEDIA • MINNEAPOLIS, MN

Imagination comes alive in Express!
Transform the everyday into the fresh and
new, discover ways to stir up flavor and
excitement, and experiment with new
ideas and materials. Express! makerspace
books: where your next creative
adventure begins!

This edition first published in 2024 by Bellwether Media, Inc.

No part of this publication may be reproduced in whole or in part without written permission of the publisher.
For information regarding permission, write to Bellwether Media, Inc., Attention: Permissions Department,
6012 Blue Circle Drive, Minnetonka, MN 55343.

Library of Congress Cataloging-in-Publication Data

Names: Burns, Kylie, author.
Title: Coding with outer space / by Kylie Burns.
Description: Minneapolis, MN : Bellwether Media, 2024. | Series: Express! Adventures in unplugged coding |
    Includes bibliographical references and index. | Audience: Ages 7-13 | Audience: Grades 4-6 |
    Summary: "Information accompanies instructions for various outer-space-themed activities that demonstrate skills
    needed for coding. The text level and subject matter are intended for students in grades 3 through 8"
    -- Provided by publisher.
Identifiers: LCCN 2023021998 (print) | LCCN 2023021999 (ebook) | ISBN 9798886875157 (library binding) |
    ISBN 9798886875652 (paperback) | ISBN 9798886877038 (ebook)
Subjects: LCSH: Computer programming--Juvenile literature. | Outer space--Juvenile literature.
Classification: LCC QA76.6115 .B873 2024 (print) | LCC QA76.6115 (ebook) | DDC 005.1--dc23/eng/20230524
LC record available at https://lccn.loc.gov/2023021998
LC ebook record available at https://lccn.loc.gov/2023021999

Editors: Sarah Eason and Christina Leaf
Illustrator: Eric Smith
Series Design: Brittany McIntosh
Graphic Designer: Paul Myerscough

Printed in the United States of America, North Mankato, MN.

TABLE OF CONTENTS _ □ X

WHAT IS UNPLUGGED CODING? _ □ X

Coding is the system that people use to **communicate** with computers. It is a way to give **commands** to a computer in a language that it understands. Computers cannot think for themselves, so programmers write **code** to give instructions in a way that computers understand.

The computer onboard the Voyager 1 spacecraft was programmed to communicate with Earth.

Unplugged coding uses many of the same skills as coding with a computer. The difference is that you can do these activities without a computer!
The unplugged activities in this book will help you develop skills that are out of this world!
For extra fun, we will use outer space as our theme.

LET'S GET STARTED!

SPACE PUDDING

In this activity, we will learn about **algorithms**. An algorithm is a set of instructions that works a little like a recipe. Each step must be written carefully and in the right order. If one step is missing or is out of order, a computer will not do the task correctly, or at all! Your mission is to follow the algorithm to make a pudding that can be eaten by astronauts in space.

YOU WILL NEED:

_ □ X

- a small zip-top sandwich bag
- pudding powder in a flavor of your choice
- a tablespoon
- a teaspoon
- a measuring cup
- powdered milk
- water
- scissors

LET'S TRY IT OUT!

1

Put 1 tablespoon plus 2 teaspoons of dry pudding powder into a zip-top bag.

2

Add 1 tablespoon plus 2 teaspoons of powdered milk.

6

3 Shake the mixture.

4 Use a measuring cup to measure just below 1/2 cup of water, and pour the water into the bag.

5 Seal the bag tightly!

6 When the bag is sealed, squish and squeeze the pudding mixture until it is completely blended and starts to thicken.

7 Cut off the corner of the bag, and squeeze the pudding into your mouth! Yum!

TURN THE PAGE TO SEE HOW YOU DID!

CHECK IT OUT!

How did your space pudding turn out? Was it difficult to follow the algorithm step by step? Were there any steps that you skipped? How did it taste?

DID YOU KNOW?

There is no gravity in outer space, so astronauts have had to create algorithms even for simple activities. For example, they have algorithms for brushing their teeth and making a sandwich. Imagine trying to spread peanut butter and jelly on a floating piece of bread!

HERE'S A TIP!

In coding, an algorithm describes how to do something step by step through commands that a computer recognizes. Find out for yourself how important getting the steps right really is. Try rearranging the steps in the pudding recipe and see what happens!

CODING CHALLENGE! _ □ X

An alien has just arrived on Earth! You must create an algorithm that teaches the alien how to brush its teeth. What steps would you give it, and in what order? Have a friend pretend to be the alien and test out your algorithm.

Coding must be **accurate**. When writing lines of code, programmers carefully choose each number, letter, word, or **symbol** to get the results they want. If just one small part of the code is wrong or left out, then there is a **bug** in the code and the program will fail. **Debugging** is a process of **analyzing** code and correcting errors so that programs will run properly.

YOU WILL NEED: _ □ X

- sharp eyesight!

LOOK CLOSELY!

DID YOU KNOW?

Bugs in a program can lead to major mistakes! In 1962, a space robot called Mariner 1 was sent into space to find out more about the planet Venus. However, just after it launched, a bug in the code sent the robot off course. The robot had to be destroyed.

Can you spot the bugs, or differences, in this pair of aliens to debug the code?

TURN THE PAGE TO SEE HOW YOU DID!

11

CHECK IT OUT!

How did you do? Were you able to identify all of the differences between the aliens? Were some differences easier to identify than others? Did your eyes go buggy in the hunt for bugs?!

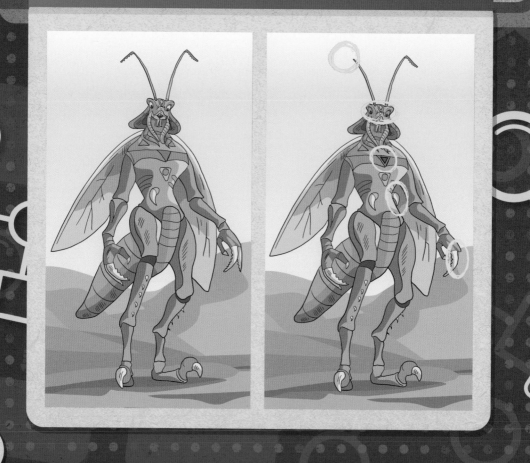

HERE'S A TIP!

When you are debugging, pay close attention to everything. Try to notice even the smallest changes. That can make the difference between a code that works and one that fails.

CODING CHALLENGE!

_ □ **X**

Try drawing two pictures that are exactly the same. Next, create a bug that very slightly changes the look of one of your pictures. Then show it to someone and see if they can debug your picture.

SPACE RACE!   _ □ X

Sequencing is an important part of creating algorithms. Sequences are step-by-step instructions for a computer program. Computers can carry out a task only if the commands are in the correct order. Understanding which steps go in which order is the key to avoiding mistakes.

Build a paper rocket using the steps in this sequenced activity! Make sure that you follow the steps in sequence!

GET READY FOR BLAST OFF!

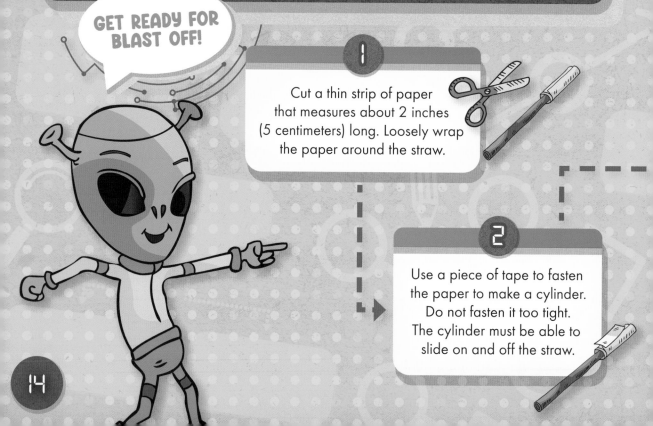

1

Cut a thin strip of paper that measures about 2 inches (5 centimeters) long. Loosely wrap the paper around the straw.

2

Use a piece of tape to fasten the paper to make a cylinder. Do not fasten it too tight. The cylinder must be able to slide on and off the straw.

3

Fold one end of the paper cylinder and tape it into the shape of a triangle. This will be the top of the rocket.

4

Take another piece of paper, and cut two corners off to form two triangles. These will be the tail pieces for your rocket.

5

Use tape to attach the tail pieces to the end of the rocket on either side. Make sure that they do not block the opening on the bottom of the rocket.

6

Try out your rocket! Place the open end onto the straw. Then, blow air through the other end of the straw to launch the rocket.

LET'S SEE HOW YOU DID!

DID YOU KNOW?

Today, computers can follow billions of commands in just 1 second!

CHECK IT OUT!

Did you manage to launch your rocket? Did it fly high, or far? How difficult was it to follow the steps in sequence? Is there anything you would do differently to improve the results?

HERE'S A TIP!

Computers cannot do things on their own. Programmers must write instructions that include every little step the computer must follow to complete a task.

CODING CHALLENGE!

＿ □ X

Go outside and have more fun with the rocket you made. Tie one end of a piece of string to a hula hoop. Have an adult help you tie the other end to a tree branch. Stand on one side of the hula hoop and shoot your rocket through the hoop. Repeat the action a few more times. Each time, increase the distance between where you stand and the hula hoop. Does your rocket make it to the other side? How far away can you stand?

TO INFINITY AND BEYOND!

Conditionals in coding involve choices. If something occurs, then another action happens as a result. Computers cannot make their own choices, so conditionals tell the computer what to do in several different situations. Computer **apps** and programs run smoothly when conditionals are used.

YOU WILL NEED: _ □ X

- a jump rope or a long piece of string
- some creative movement ideas

If you want to try conditionals, then try this game! Ask a friend to play with you. Imagine that one person is a space explorer who has just landed on the planet Mars. The other person is a Martian. Take turns being the Martian and the space explorer.

LET'S TRY IT OUT!

DID YOU KNOW?

Programmers can also create conditionals for computer apps that determine what is shown on the screen. This includes graphics such as images and text. It also includes characters, actions, and background colors.

1. Place the jump rope or piece of string on the floor. Make sure that it is in a straight line.
2. Each person must stand on opposite sides of the rope or string, facing each other.
3. Next, the Martian says "Do this." They then carry out several different actions in a short algorithm. For example, wave one arm, jump up, and turn around.
4. The space explorer tries to copy each command in the algorithm, exactly as the Martian did them.

Conditional:

If the Martian does not say "Do this" before doing the actions, and the space explorer copies them, then the Martian wins. However, if the space explorer remains still, then the space explorer wins. The faster the game is played, the harder it becomes!

LET'S SEE HOW YOU DID!

How did the conditionals work for you? Did you find it difficult to follow several commands in a row? Did you focus on waiting for the words "Do this," or were you more focused on getting the actions right?

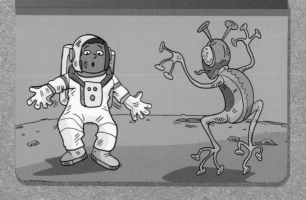

HERE'S A TIP!

Conditionals are read as "true" or "false" statements by computers. If a condition is true, then a particular result occurs. If it is false, then another result occurs, or nothing happens at all. It is like a chain reaction!

CODING CHALLENGE! _ □ X

Pretend you are the captain of a spaceship. Your friends are astronauts stranded on the moon with no way home. But you have room in your spaceship for only one passenger! You will need a jump rope for this activity.

1. Lay a jump rope down on the ground in a straight line. Everyone stands behind it.
2. The captain takes 10 large steps forward from the line and stops, but does not turn around.
3. The captain yells out a conditional statement, such as, "If your shirt is blue, then walk forward 3 steps," or "If you like to eat broccoli, then hop forward once."
4. The captain calls out conditionals until an astronaut makes it past the captain, winning the last spot on the spaceship!

I HOPE YOU ENJOYED UNPLUGGED CODING!

21

GLOSSARY _ □ X

accurate—correct and without mistakes

algorithms—step-by-step methods to solve a problem

analyzing—looking carefully at something to understand how it works and its important parts

apps—programs such as games or internet browsers; an app is also called an application.

bug—a coding error in a program

code—instructions for a computer

commands—specific instructions to complete a task

communicate—to share knowledge or information

conditionals—lines of programming language that allow different actions depending on true or false information; conditionals are often written in IF/THEN statements.

debugging—finding and removing mistakes in code

sequencing—the process of putting a set of instructions in a certain order

symbol—a shape that has a meaning

TO LEARN MORE

AT THE LIBRARY

Gater, Will. *The Mysteries of the Universe*. New York, N.Y.: DK Publishing, 2020.

Hutt, Sarah. *Crack the Code!: Activities, Games, and Puzzles That Reveal the World of Coding*. New York, N.Y.: Penguin Workshop, 2018.

Prottsman, Kiki. *How to Be a Coder*. New York, N.Y.: DK Publishing, 2019.

ON THE WEB

FACTSURFER

Factsurfer.com gives you a safe, fun way to find more information.

1. Go to www.factsurfer.com.

2. Enter "coding with outer space" into the search box and click 🔍.

3. Select your book cover to see a list of related content.

INDEX _ □ X